Contemplations of a Bandaged Soul

A Memoir and Other Thoughts Told Through Essays

By

Vera Padgett

1

To O.T.

To Lila, my grandmother.

Table of Contents

God's First Daughter, Not Man's Second Thought

Woman was God's last creation. Nothing was created in order of value, one must understand that. Women were not created last because we are to be "subservient to Man," but rather because we are the crown of creation. Not even the angels were present when Woman was created. It was a holy moment nothing else was given the privilege of having, and God gave it to us.

God put Adam to sleep and took one of his ribs to make Eve. Eve was not made from the dirt under Adam's feet, nor was she made from the air above his head. She was made from his rib, which is what protects our vital organs. Eve was made to be at the side of Adam and protect his heart. She protects him and he protects her.

If I could tell you exactly which point in time where we forgot that fact, I would. But there really is not one single moment where we started viewing women as less than what God made us to be. So many factors go into it, such as cultural views, especially in regions where Christians are a tiny minority. When it is the cultural norm to treat women with the same rights as farm animals and it has been that way for millennia, of course it is going to get ingrained into both men and women that women only exist to serve the men.

It is not a lie that Christendom is afflicted by this sorry excuse for behavior as well. Again, I have no idea who exactly is responsible, only that they have a lot to answer for. Free will plays a very large part in it too, though; nastiness toward people can get inherited just as easily as tradition. Sometimes, nastiness *is* the tradition.

Setting that aside for a moment, I need to explain something about some of the women in the Old Testament. As much as I love all the righteous women in the Bible, I am tired of Ruth being the only one us women are called to be like in church. Ruth was a woman of exceptional patience and love, which are two of the fruits of the Holy Spirit. But not every woman is naturally inclined to be exactly like Ruth; many of us are like Deborah or Esther. We are not naturally quiet or "girly" as people often paint Ruth to be, but we are just as feminine as the Ruths of today because God gave us all different strengths. Where the Ruths exhibit the fruits of love, patience, kindness, and gentleness primarily, the Deborahs and Esthers exhibit goodness first and foremost. Goodness in this sense means to do what is right by God, and we see doing what is right as advocating for the vulnerable like Esther or helping to lead the charge against our enemies like Deborah. All of these women are righteous because they did precisely what God wanted them specifically to do and did not tamp down parts of themselves to fit a pretty little mold that is wrongly labeled "one size fits all." You are feminine precisely because you are a woman, not because you subscribe to the outward aesthetic that femininity has become. If you are naturally loud and jovial, be loud and jovial. If you are naturally quick-witted, be quick-witted. You can serve God without changing yourself.

Allow me to paint the pictures of these three different Godly women, none greater than another. Just because I do not feel it is necessarily my calling to be married or have children at this point in my life–God may change that but there is nothing scandalous about not wanting marriage or children–does not mean I dislike Ruth. My only gripe–which is a very personal one–that I am outlining here is that many Christian women's groups are like grown-up tea parties; instead of girls talking about Prince Charming, it is now women "waiting for their Boaz" and talking about nothing but daydreams of marriage. It is often laid on very thick that the best thing a woman can do is get married to a good man and have children. But that can sometimes spit in the face of other courageous women in the Bible and our own Saints, such as Joan of Arc and St. Agatha as well as women like me who are afflicted with incurable illnesses and may never be well enough to have children–not because we feel we

8

need to be offended by every little thing, but because we have been treated as broken for not being able to carry a child or not feeling like marriage is what we are called to do. If it is a part of God's specific plan for you to marry and have children, that is an absolutely wonderful thing and I hope you find the utmost fulfillment from it. But I know that I am not accomplishing less by staying celibate and/or not having children if I do get married; God's specific plan requires something different from me.

In the Book of Ruth, Naomi's sons die and Orpah, one of Naomi's daughters-in-law, leaves for her homeland. Ruth refuses to leave Naomi. In Ruth 1:16-17, Ruth says "Don't urge me to leave you or to turn back from you. Where you go I will go, and where you stay I will stay. Your people will be my people and your God my God. Where you die I will die, and there I will be buried. May the Lord deal with me, be it ever so severely, if even death separates you and me." Ruth's loyalty to Naomi and her courage to go with her to a land she has never known is so significant, and so is how she treats Boaz and the others in the barley fields. She is noted for her humility even when Boaz blesses her and grants her protection. That is what Ruth's story should be about, not just highlighting that she got married and had Obed, who was the grandfather of David. A woman's value does not come from the possibly great and powerful future generations that come from her children, it comes from how she treats others. She was loyal to Naomi who had lost everything and was bitter that the Lord had afflicted her, and she was humble with Boaz who had ensured she would not be harmed, that she was fed, and that she brought back grain to Naomi. Regardless of if another person has everything or has lost everything, we should not let that stop us from treating people with the utmost kindness and respect.

Esther was Jewish and became the Queen of Persia. She hid her Jewish identity during the pageant when the King of Persia chose her to be his new queen. The first time Esther came to the king with information, it was when Mordecai overheard two guards plotting to kill the king. But the second time, she risked her own life to protect her people. Is this not one of the noblest things one can do? Mordecai refused to kneel to Haman, so Haman went to the king and told him to kill all the Jews, since they did not follow Persian law. Mordecai urged Esther to tell the king of her identity so the Jews would be safe, but she was afraid. Mordecai told her in Esther 4:13-14: "Do not imagine that you in the king's palace can escape any more than all the other Jews. For if you keep silent at this time, liberation and rescue will arise for the Jews from another place, and you and your father's house will perish. And who knows whether you have not attained royalty for such a time as this?" Esther replied, telling Mordecai to go tell the Jews to fast and pray for 3 days and then said, "If I perish, I perish." When our femininity is reduced to mid twentieth-century advertisements and postcards showing us cleaning or cooking and doing nothing else, we forget about women like Esther who almost certainly faced death and did what they had to do anyway.

It is also worth mentioning that God is not mentioned at all in the Book of Esther. That does not mean He is not there, it simply shows how God is still always working even when it does not seem like He is. Mordecai suggesting that perhaps Esther being made Queen of Persia for a time when her people would be persecuted was a part of God's plan is indicative of that. Esther came to the king and told him of Haman's plot and of her own identity. The king was outraged, but not with her–with Haman. He ordered Haman to be hanged, and allowed the Jews to defend themselves from their enemies. If Esther had instead chosen to remain silent, in the same way so many women are urged to be so as to not "cause problems," she along with her people would have died.

Deborah, as my last example, was married and was still a prophetess and judge. That is part of why I am using her as an example of what service to God might look like. Many Israelites came to her to settle their disputes. She did not stay inside her house and bake bread all day or nurse her children long after they needed her milk, she was out under her own palm tree assisting her community. God spoke through her and she gave a message to Barak: he will lead ten thousand people to Mount Tabor while God leads Sisera to the Kishon River and directly into Barak's hands. Barak did not disregard her, he listened. Why did he listen? Because he knew God was speaking through Deborah and understood God will use whoever He needs to do His will. Barak replied that he would go if Deborah came with him. She agreed, telling him that the honor of battle will be the Lord's and not Barak's. The Lord would deliver Sisera into the hands of a woman, and Barak did not snicker at that.

The woman Sisera was delivered to was not Deborah, but Jael. Sisera had seen the army of ten thousand advancing and leapt off his horse, fleeing on foot to Jael's tent as his army was slaughtered. She had let him in and, while he was sleeping, stabbed him through the temple with a tent spike. Barak had found her tent and Jael let him in, showing him Sisera's lifeless body. We do not ever say Jael or Deborah were too masculine, do we?

Additionally, apart from her story in the Book of Judges, it is not definitively known if Deborah had biological children. But it is written in Judges 5:7 that she was a "mother in Israel;" a spiritual mother to her nation. When Ruth is shown as our only example of a biblically righteous woman, it only gives us one of many different paths God may intend for our lives to go. Many women glorify God by marrying righteous men and having children to raise in the faith, and that is a very beautiful and holy thing. But God might not pave that path for *every* woman. The Deborahs among us might be called to be *spiritual* mothers: not necessarily having biological children of their own, but being like mothers toward people who need them the most. Being a spiritual guide to someone and influencing them to take steps toward God is, in some cases, our fulfillment as mothers.

Populating Heaven–not just Earth–must be our shared goal, in whatever way God intends for us to do so. Some will go on to become wonderful mothers and their families will remember their legacy forever. Some will go on to help the brokenhearted and forgotten and show them divine love. Others will step up to lead the righteous against evil. Whatever God calls you to do, do it, and do it well! We are God's daughters, and we must act like it!

For Such a Time As This

In the last essay, I wrote about Ruth, Esther, and Deborah. I would like to talk about Esther more and relate Mordecai's words to her to a part of my own life story.

I was not protected by my family–grandparents excluded–like I should have been. Starting when I was eight years old, I began to be sexually abused by a boy four years older than me who lived across the street. I no longer pace and obsess over why he targeted me of all people, because there is not an attainable answer to that. The only answer that matters is that it was not my fault.

Some people can remember down to the hour when their abuse started. I cannot, and that is alright. I do not remember if it was summer or during the school year, but I am almost certain it was the latter. I remember how all of the kids in the neighborhood that rode the same bus to elementary school would meet on our street to play with toy guns that shot foam bullets. We would bring our best ones and put them in a pile to share, borrowing them from each other. One day, just as ordinary as the rest, my abuser, Ryan (as much as I would love to say his full name, that would have legal repercussions, but I'll say his first name), decided he wanted to form a club of some sort. The initiation to get in was simply a high-five for every kid but me, of course. He took me aside and asked, "Do you want to be a part of the club?" Of course I said yes.

"Follow me behind the houses to where the hedges are," he replied.

He took me back there and told me to give him oral sex, that was my initiation into the club. My mother had told me before that if anyone told me to do anything like that with them, I was to say no. So I said no. That did not deter him. His coaxing turned into insisting, which turned into threatening. I was very afraid; I was doing everything my mom told me to do! Why was he still asking?

So I did it. I hated it, but I did it. Again, I am not writing this to relive it or think of all the things I could have done differently, because it was not my fault. I am blameless, I was eight years old. To anyone who says "well, what was that little tramp wearing," when a woman is assaulted, I was wearing my school uniform: a polo shirt and a skirt with built-in shorts underneath. Was that immodest enough to warrant molestation?

This is the first time I am ever writing this story out in detail. I find now that it is unpleasant to write, of course, but I do not feel like I am eight again–I know I am safe. Praise the Lord.

These secret meetings near the hedges where I would be made to take him into my mouth–and other things that I will not say because they are far too explicit and horrifying when children are involved– went on every day after school for nearly three years. I believe I was almost eleven when it all ended. This might sound odd, but it is wholly true: I have two computer games to thank for helping me put distance between Ryan and me. Once I started spending more time inside playing those games, Ryan finally stopped coming around and asking about me. He moved away a few months after that, maybe a year after.

When it comes to childhood trauma, your mind protects you from things you legitimately cannot process with an underdeveloped brain by "forgetting." Most of it gets stored in the back of your mind and is given what-for with a black marker so you cannot see what is underneath. But when you are older, the marker gets erased. In my case, I was thirteen years old sitting in my eighth grade science class. We were watching one of those short safety films for students that will be going into high school and learning about what harassment is, what it looks like, and what to do if it happens. We were watching a skit about sexual harassment, and that's when the marker on my memories got erased. I had to grip the sides of my desk to keep from crying or screaming. I had to breathe deeply to keep from throwing up. Two and a half years worth of memories of sexual abuse hit me all at once.

I spent the next two years trying to grapple with these memories. Looking back, I did very well. I was trying my best with no professional mental help that I badly needed and I just focused on channeling my emotions into loud music or, at the time, tarot cards. I was still a witch at that time. Either way, I did not do half bad just trying to survive.

That brings me to today. Well, in a literal sense, a few months ago. I was at church–my usual evening service that suits my health needs–and the sermon was interactive in a way. The priest asked us all various questions and gave us time to write down our answers silently. They were decently engaging, and then he got to one of the last questions, if not the last one. He asked us, "What is something that God has saved you from in your life?"

It was a good question. I thought about it for a moment, and then it dawned on me for the first time in my life that God had saved me from getting pregnant at eight years old. A memory came back to me at that moment: Ryan had asked me one day if he could use my body in a certain way that biologically runs the risk of a pregnancy. He obviously did not say it like that, I am only writing it that way for the sake of making this chapter readable. I had unrestricted internet access at that age, and I knew the risk of doing what he was asking, so I very adamantly said no, that was something that I would *never* let him do. He went on with his usual "Oh, come on, don't be like that," and I again said no. And then the only time he ever did the following happened; he conceded. He grumbled, yes, but he never asked again. He was not the type to do that, to just stop pestering. I realized that in church.

For someone who is abusive to actually listen to you and not do something you do not want them to do, that is God doing work around you. It is like part of my life came crashing down almost in a good way —if that makes sense—because I realized that even in that trauma where I was being treated like a toy, God was still simultaneously shielding me from worse harm *and* working on his heart. I cried the whole way home from church, thanking God for not letting the unthinkable happen. The fact that I had to consider the risk of pregnancy at only eight years old was bad enough.

When Esther was filled with fear over the idea of telling the King of Persia herself that she was a Jew and that it was her people that were going to be killed, Mordecai told her: "Perhaps you were made queen for such a time as this." She could have very easily said, "I wish I was never made queen, I don't want to be in any more danger," but she did not. She knew Mordecai was suggesting that God's plans and the points He makes within our lives are far more perfectly timed than we can imagine. That does not mean you should go around telling people in the depths of their grief that they need to cheer up because God is with them! It's a terrible thing to say "everything happens for a reason," when someone is going through the inconceivable.

The conclusion that we too were made to go through specific experiences "for such a time as this" is one that needs to be found by the *individual,* through God, on their own time. It is not at all something you can just tell someone; God will tell them that Himself. If someone had told me at fifteen or sixteen that I went through all that sexual abuse for years for a reason, I would have knocked their teeth out. Even though I know now that God is specifically using my past experiences as part of my spiritual growth today, years ago would have been the wrong time to tell me that–I was just trying to survive back then. That is a message God has to show each of us when He knows the time is right. If you have not seen someone's entire life, you do not get to make that choice.

Two of my biggest "for such a time as this" moments have been my sexual abuse and the grief and trauma of having a father who only cares about women if he can have adult relations, to say the least, with them. Which means he does not care about me, his daughter. And that is okay. I do not know how to explain that to someone; it took me years to get to a point where I can say that if he genuinely does not want me around, I am not wasting my time. In all honesty, he does look a lot like King Henry VIII anyway. I wish I was joking, but I am terribly serious. He looks like him and acts like him. Why cry over a man like that?

I bring up my father because how a father treats his daughter is, in most cases, the treatment his daughter will unconsciously seek out in a future boyfriend or husband. If all you know is being abandoned or shouted at, and you do not know what peaceful and patient love looks like, how are you supposed to know any better when another man charms his way into your life and then lies to you? That is why I do not think I shall marry. I do not hate men, and I do not hate marriage. If I did hate men, I would be hating God because men are made in the image of God. The same goes for men who hate women. And marriage is so holy, but it is also a lifelong commitment. If you are hesitant, you do not have to get married until you know for sure whether you want to or not.

I do not want to get married. And that is okay! God gave me a gift for writing and I want to keep practicing and getting better at it all the time. The Holy Spirit is guiding me to write this book now. If my dad had not been the way he was and I was married by now or soon to be married, I would not have rediscovered my love of writing and I never would have thought that I could ever write any book worth its salt. If I had not experienced all that I have experienced, I would have no idea how to tell people how much God has done for me. Perhaps my life has gone the way it has for such a time as this.

Lessons From the Cemetery

When I was young and my parents were freshly divorced, my grandmother would pick me up after school each day and take me to the cemetery. Some of her family was buried there, and she would make sure the dead leaves didn't cover their headstones and obscure their identities. We'd have math lessons there, she'd point out a headstone and say "Tell me how old they were when they died," in her warm Southern drawl. I'd take note of their birth year and figure out how many years had passed until their death year, tacking off one year as needed if they hadn't yet reached their birthday. It was a quiet afternoon ritual, and it was uniquely ours.

We got into the habit of this after-school tending to the dead for a few years. After a while, I felt comfortable enough to ask questions about these people who had died, even if neither of us knew the person. I assumed since my grandmother was so wise and knew the answers to all of my silly, naive questions, she'd also have the answers to my questions about the deaths of the people labeled on the headstones. But that was one thing she didn't have the answers to. Not only that, she was content not to have them.

This was the moment when I got my first lessons in the Protestant Christian view of the afterlife. It was also when she taught me that death was a natural thing and that it could even be very beautiful. My family was never the kind to keep the fact of death away from children; it was never a taboo topic. And it shouldn't be! Death is difficult to talk about, but it needs to be talked about. I remember when I'd ask her "How did they die?" and point to a headstone, and she'd just shrug and reply, "I don't know, I didn't know them."

"Did they go to Heaven?"

"I'm not sure. It's not for us to decide who goes to Heaven or Hell, only God knows. And you can't tell just by looking at someone or their headstone in the cemetery."

"What happens when we die?"

One thing you must know about me is that I was a very inquisitive young girl, and I often asked very large questions. But my grandmother didn't mind. She had a way of answering my questions honestly and without any sugar coating, but also without harshness or bluntness. She informed me but did not scare me.

"We won't really know what happens when we die until we get there. The act of dying is not scary, and it doesn't hurt. Your soul goes to Heaven, but your body stays here on earth. It's like letting go of a ball and watching it bounce down a hill; the ball is still yours, you're just not holding onto it anymore."

A moment of silence passed as her words sunk into my naive mind.

"Are these people missed, just like you miss your Grammie?"

I called my grandmother "Grammie," so it only made sense to me that her grandmother was also Grammie.

"Oh, I'm sure they are. I hope they have sweet little granddaughters to come visit them, too."

What she didn't tell me at that time is that you don't learn what grief is beyond the dictionary definition until someone you love dies. When that happens, you realize that the "five stages of grief" aren't stages, but waters you travel between like a stranded fishing boat against its will. I am not sure if that journey ever really ends once it has started, but I can tell you that once you've drifted through the same seas for so long, you can map out the ports you've docked at before and can see the lighthouses even through cloudy nights. At one point you can even throw away your map, you'll be able to navigate without it. Grief gets easier to accept; I just had to learn that all very quickly once she suddenly had an accident.

My grandmother hadn't even been taking her chemotherapy pills for a week in 2022 before she had a massive stroke, her blood pressure had climbed so high. It really was an act of God that it was a Saturday morning and my grandfather was up quite early to get ready to go fishing. Had he not been around or left later, I would've been the one to find her on her bedroom floor when I went over to visit at 10 AM.

"You know, in Proverbs, it says that we are not promised tomorrow. It's nothing to be scared about, God knows what He's doing. We just have to be ready and willing to go when that time comes. You can't fight God and win."

I realize now as I'm writing this that when she told me that all those years ago, she wasn't just teaching me about the Bible. She was teaching me how to navigate life without fear. The wonderful people who were close to her can tell you, that she had such a wisdom about her and her calmness in so many situations was astounding. When she was in that hospice bed, I remember that no words were going through my brain. Only tears were coming out of my eyes. I remember being very sad and overwhelmed as I felt like I was being forced to prepare for a lifetime without her. But now I can look back and know that she was still there with me even while unconscious. She was silently giving me her own final goodbyes on this earth because I felt an odd undercurrent of calmness and acceptance despite not wanting her to go, just like she had taught me to do in every situation. "It's nothing to be scared about, God knows what He's doing. We just have to be ready and willing to go when that time comes." That was the second and final time she told me that in the only way she could, and I thank her for it.

One final very important thing that she taught me was that life is not always going to be kind to us. We are going to suffer in our lives, and we must accept that. "Nowhere in the Bible does it say that we are required to sit around and wallow in our pity while we feel sorry for ourselves. It does say to rejoice always, though. We are to praise the Lord all the time, even when the times are tough. The suffering on earth is still a part of God's plan," my grandmother would tell me. I suppose for some odd reason I'd never have to apply that to her death. But that was a foolish thought for me to have because she was the one who told me that death was a natural thing in the first place.

It took me a long time to be able to see that she went home with perfect timing. I was heavily saddened and even felt burdened by her passing, but I was and am still grateful that the Lord took her when He did and didn't prolong her suffering any longer than what was necessary. The best thing I can do to honor her memory is to practice everything she taught me while she was able to; she was the one who turned quiet and somber cemetery visits into learning experiences and fond memories, and I find that even in tiny, everyday experiences I am drawn back to her.

Her knowledge will see me through my life until I return to the cemetery to stay. After that, I'm not worried. God knows what He's doing.

Proverbs 27:1 - "Do not boast about tomorrow, for you do not know what any day may bring forth."

1 Thessalonians 5:16-18 - "Rejoice always. Pray without ceasing. In all circumstances give thanks, for this is the will of God for you in Christ Jesus."

The Deceptive Affliction

For the strangest reason, people seem to think grief and mourning are contagious. It's perfectly simple to see their thought process, though: "Being around someone who is so sad all the time or who keeps bringing up this dead person makes me sad. I do not want to be around them for fear of missing said deceased person, too." Many individuals don't want to dive into the swamps of bereavement because they would rather not deal with the mess of having to dry off after their swim.

But what about us who were thrown into those swamps against our will? What do we do? We were not offered the same helping hand and towel. We're still fighting off the alligators and the algae that sticks to every little part of you. Are we ever destined to find our way out, or are we to be looked at like zoo animals who are beyond help because of our perceived filth?

Perhaps we are plague patients, where grief is both the symptom and the disease. As far as you may come in your recovery, your remission will only ever be partial. Only other patients will recognize your remission; the uninfected only see that you're sick and recoil if you get too close or are symptomatic. But at the same time, grief is not contagious. It most definitely can behave like a chronic illness with its unpredictability, but you won't catch it from close contact. And that is where the deception lies. When did this natural part of the human condition become an enemy?

I believe it comes with the hurried lives many of us live. "There's just no time to grieve. I have a job, I have children to care for. I can't spend my time wallowing." Do you think that I don't feel the same? I can't fit mourning on my schedule either, yet it cancels my plans to make room for itself to lounge and then expects me to wait on it hand and foot. I have no choice in the matter, but I must obey. I am not given other options. Trust me when I say that I don't wish this on anyone else, but you must understand that there's nothing I could've done to prevent it. The notion that we who grieve seem to have done something wrong to make us act this way is absolutely and totally incorrect, and you will not do yourself any harm by slowing down to walk alongside us once in a while, either. You might learn something from us.

I am reminded of a dream I had quite a while ago. It's significant that I still remember the dream because I usually forget them soon after I wake up. In it, I was in my neighborhood subdivision, possibly taking a walk or something of the like; I remember being outside near the entrance. I saw my grandmother's car slowly drive by to the stoplight, with her driving. Even in my dream state, I knew this was an anomaly. She was dead, why was she here, driving? The light turned green, and she turned left onto the highway. She smiled and waved goodbye to me as she drove off. I was so shocked, I didn't know what to say or to do next. Where was she going? Why was she going? Why was she even there? But the most significant and symbolically powerful part of this dream was that it kept happening. I didn't move, but her car would turn left and vanish down the hill, then her car would drive from the subdivision gate to the light, and turn left once more. And she waved every single time. I called my mother over to come see Grammie driving away. She was just as astonished as I was. I believe I remember us crying in the dream, relieved to see her again and that she was okay.

This dream was a vast jump from the ones I dreamt prior with her in them. Before, she would just sit or stand there, regarding me with a neutral gaze. Not disappointed, but not her usual warm look either. Simply existing. I would reach out to hug her, and she would not reciprocate. It was like trying to hug a photograph; you absolutely could, but it wouldn't hug back. To have this dream of her smiling and acknowledging my mother and me meant a lot to me. Do I believe it was really her? Probably not. But it was a good dream for me to have because, in my mind, it symbolized letting her go onto better things. It meant that she was happy to go, and that's truly all I could've asked for.

You see, this is where grief confuses people. I have accepted my grandmother's death, and I thank God that He took her when He did. I can live my life and function day to day without being in distress, but that does not at all mean that I've "gotten over her." What a terrible thing to say to someone, to assume one can just forget about someone so unforgettable! Just because I can enjoy my days again does not mean that I don't wish my deceased loved ones could enjoy them with me. People can be so black and white in their thinking (I am one of them, I confess) that any smidge of happiness despite overwhelming emotions means you're all better. But that's not it, is it? No, they assume so because they seek the shallow comfort of denial; they just can't fathom not taking the easy way out. Their discomfort with your acceptance of tidal emotions is their issue to resolve, not yours. The longer one ignores the problem, the worse it will get.

Treat the affliction, and you'll recover. So get on with
it.

Hearts of Speech

Death is not a bad word. Dying is not derogatory. But people still treat it like it is, and insist you not say it. You're the one grieving, and there will always be someone who will say, "Saying that she died is a bit harsh, is it not? I believe saying she 'passed away' is a bit softer and easier." Softer and easier? For you, maybe. But for me she was alive, telling me she loved me and would see me tomorrow, and the next she was in hospice after a massive stroke. Don't tell me what's softer and easier, because I've already begged for softer and easier things to happen and they didn't. Death is not polite. Don't speak about it like it is.

I also have problems with the phrase "she went home to Jesus." I understand the sentiment and that it's meant to be comforting knowing that her soul is not in pain anymore, but she had a home here! Her home was across the street, where I'd sit and watch television with her for hours, and then she'd sit in the chair in her bedroom, I'd sit on her bed, and we'd talk until nearly 10 o'clock at night. *That* was her home, and it was somewhere I could go to see her anytime I wanted. Now I have to remember her through photographs, and I'm afraid I'm forgetting the sound of her voice.

The more afraid you are to say certain words pertaining to loss, the harder denial will hit you. My grandmother DIED. She is DEAD. She is NOT COMING BACK. I HAVE HER ASHES IN A NECKLACE. As she would probably say, "I ain't gonna get any deader, so don't stop living just 'cause I ain't there."

People often have the best intentions with choosing their language, but it has the opposite effect. I have dubbed this art of thinking before speaking the "Hearts of Speech." They want to empathize, so they take the time to choose their words carefully. Sometimes it really helps, and other times it makes you angry because they still sound so insensitive. Whether to brush it off or not depends on their intentions. If they mean well, it can be excused. If they don't, well, I trust you to make your own decisions. The point is that the empathy and care in a conversation after someone dies greatly diminishes when they choose to soften the blow with cute little words. The blow of the words are not as harsh as you think they are! The real blow came when my grandmother had the stroke, and I suddenly had to come to terms with the fact that she would likely not live another week and would never speak or react to my words until then! Anything you say cannot possibly be as agonizing as that was.

I wonder what she saw while in her coma. I hope it was lovely. Knowing her, she likely replayed memories of taking care of me growing up: the times we made bracelets, baked little desserts for tea parties together, even watching over me at her house when I was sick and had to stay home from school.

Maybe she saw her father. He was not a nice man on earth, but he converted to Christianity on his deathbed. She always told me she hoped he meant it and wasn't simply trying to sneak his way into Heaven, because she really wanted to see him there. I hope she got to see him, and that he was finally nice to her. I hope he was waiting in Heaven for her when she died. I don't find myself doing it as often anymore, but I used to hope she'd come back to us down here—that the door would open and I'd hear the jingle of her keys on her purse and the soft shuffle of her feet on the tile floor. That she'd come back and tell me how bad the traffic was and how the young worker at the store didn't know how to count the coins for her change. "This is the next generation of the workforce," she'd say, "and they can't count change!"

If you read only that last paragraph and then were to talk to me about her, I'm sure you'd say "She's in a better place now, and she's not sick anymore. It was God's plan." I'd agree with you. I know she is. But that doesn't mean I can't wish she was still down here. "We lost her on November 2nd." No we didn't! I know exactly where she is, and she ain't lost. She wasn't one to wander far. She was just proving the point she always made: people are most likely to die within a month of their birthday. Hers was October 2nd.

Isaiah 57:1 - "The righteous perish, and no one takes it to heart; the devout are taken away, and no one understands that the righteous are taken away to be spared from evil."

The Weight of Loneliness

Alcohol, nicotine, and other drugs don't replace the need for human connection built on deep trust—I've tried them. They are no distraction, only gasoline on a fire. And love is not a want, it's a need. I want to be held by a man throughout the night. But I don't have any man I love in that way, nor do I currently trust any man well enough to do that without him trying to pull something else. I want a hug from my grandmother. That was the last time I was properly held, and it's approaching 3 years without her. She would sit and hold me and rub my back for as long as I needed her to. She never asked questions about why I needed a hug, she only recognized she was needed. Love without strings attached is too rare these days, whether the strings are lust where there should be romance, or death where there should be life.

I'm cold. I'm tired. I feel empty. It's 4 o'clock in the morning and I can't sleep. I feel like I'm mindlessly drifting through a cold, rocky place. There's fog everywhere and I can hardly see my hands in front of me. What should I do? Where do I go? Are there others that pass through here, too?

<center>~~~~~~~~~~~~~~~~~~~~~~~~~~~~~~~~~~~~~~</center>

I must confess, I forgot about this piece. I remember the night I wrote it, but I never touched it again until now. It was late, and getting the ache out of my heart at the time was only to help me sleep. But I will continue it, because I remember the point I was trying to make. I was trying to say that the world—whether it's Satan, men, or both—has convinced us that "the next big thing" is better than anything you can get from another person. Love, validation, laughter? You can get that online. But more than that, the world actively discourages you from turning off the Internet, albeit in sneaky ways. Right as you're about to log off and go to bed, you get an advertisement for a product you just can't live without. Right as you're about to turn off the phone to greet your family members who've just arrived for Christmas, you see the video you've been trying to find for ages. For most of us, that'll be as far as it goes.

But for some, through whatever reason is personal to them, it goes much further than that. Addiction, greed, lust, whatever the vice—some people are sold the premium package of filling the void. I am not saying this to speak poorly about addicts. Addiction starts for so many different reasons, and it is never as simple as "just quitting." Addiction rewires the brain and makes quitting feel physically impossible, and for some people it is; it kills them. That is why they deserve tenfold as much patience and love as the rest of us get.

I'd say that these issues are a growing problem, but that would imply that they're new. They aren't; society just recycles the same script every few decades to hide that they've been failing those in need for millennia. There is a pandemic of heartlessness upon this earth that has been here since ancient times and we're being played for fools by those in power. They know we so easily turn to fighting each other over the simplest things.

And none of those options are a solution. They only serve to divide us more—see the people fighting in the streets and breaking into shops and homes after natural disasters to steal. That is the fruit of an atheistic society that has been taught to value the ego over selflessness. Every matter is "mine, mine, mine," and there is no room for disagreement. But under all of that anger and selfishness, there is a deep, throbbing loneliness. There is a desperate want to be a part of something. If the heart cannot find that through respectable means, it will find it anywhere it can—like in a gang—or it will reject it altogether and isolate itself.

There *is* a sort of balm for the heart that can soothe even the most wounded, but it requires a detoxification from the ways of the world. How can one heal if they continue to injure themselves?

That balm I mentioned is Christ. He always has been and always will be the most effective treatment for our basic, deep-seated need for love and acceptance in an animalistic world. This is what I was eventually going to reference when I wrote, "Are there others that pass through here, too?" Yes, others pass through, but you may never see each other. Sometimes you'll catch someone waving at you and you'll wave back, but then you're both led in different directions. Sometimes you will see someone being led down a path by a hand you may not recognize anymore; God leads your path, but who leads theirs? You may be offered a shortcut that you know is dangerous. You decline, then end up on a safer path and watch the ground crumble beneath the other person at the edge of a cliff. When this happens, don't be smug. Pray for them, they might not have known they were going that way. It very well could have been you had you not known that way was weak ground.

Some at this point will likely ask if life gets easier once you become a Christian. The short and long answers are both "absolutely not." Life does not get easier, but it can get *simpler.* Suffering may not ease for you, it hasn't for me. Maybe someday it will. But the simplicity comes in knowing that my entire life is but a moment in the grand scale, and suffering is a bodily thing. It may not always be physical, it can be mental or emotional. But when the body dies, if God calls us His good and faithful servant, that suffering stays in the ground. It doesn't follow us to Heaven. When you suffer, look up. If Heaven is where you aim, the angels will join you in carrying your burdens.

Chronic Migraine

Quiet! Quiet! Quiet!

I need quiet! Why does no one care? Why does no one listen?

Stomp, stomp, stomping through the house, shouting at the top of their lungs to have a conversation standing a foot away from each other.

The sun needs to dim itself down, I tell you. Much too bright. Even with this ice pack covering my forehead and eyes, it's still too bright.

Ah, the ice pack. That's the one thing that helps when I'm like this. The cold gives me something to focus on. But even so, if the migraine attack lasts well into the night, the ice pack will be warm when I wake up.

Don't do this to me! How am I to go back to sleep if I have no relief?

When I get like that, cold, in pain, and utterly alone in the dark, I cry. I turn into a child again. I want my mommy. I want my daddy. Somebody, somebody safe to hold me and make sure I make it through the night. Yes, I know that I am not in danger of dying from my typical attacks. But when I hurt that badly, and for so many years (I am approaching my 7th year of this nightmare), I almost wish it *was* terminal.

At 16, I would walk over to my bedroom wall and stare at it. How hard could I bash my head against it to get the pain to stop?

Calling insurance. Please hold. All of our available associates are busy. Please hold. Please hold. I'm sorry, we cannot approve your medication. You don't meet the medical criteria. Yes, I understand, I see on your file that you have been on these medications for years. But it's just our policy, we cannot make exceptions.

I'm only 22. I should be having fun with my friends. I should have a job or be in college, meeting people, and learning how to be independent. My days should be sunny and free. These are the best years of my life.

These are the best years of my life.

The best years of my life, spent fighting for medicine and trying to get nerve blocks for my pain. I don't care what gets approved. I will try anything. If you wanted to peel my nerves out of my body like string cheese without anesthesia, I'd let you. It would probably hurt less than the attacks.

I am exhausted. I have said this many times since I was 14, for many different reasons, but it's still true: my body may be young, but I feel 100. I feel as if I've lived enough for the next 3 generations after me. And sometimes, yes, I'm ready to die. I wouldn't dare go on anything other than God's timing, I might get into big trouble for that. That would be worse than the migraine.

God? I know you're there. I feel your presence when I'm lying in bed, shivering, sweating, and trying not to throw up. I try to take that time to pray, and it's very good that you know my thoughts. Whispering is too daunting. I pray in my head. Sometimes I am so focused on my pain that I forget to. I know you take care of me, I notice it all the time. I just wish you could physically be here. Mama doesn't understand. Bubba does a little, but not quite. It's complicated for him to understand things fully if he hasn't experienced them. I can be the same way.

I read about St. Therese of Lisieux last night. If St. Dymphna wasn't already my patron saint, I think Therese would be. She had tuberculosis and died at age 24. I think if I reach 24, it shall be a hard year. I will think about her. Maybe I'll be able to make a pilgrimage. Her Little Way is very nice to practice. It reminds me to not look for signs that God is there, but to trust that He is. It helps me to imagine Him in a grand, ornate chair by my bedside, watching over me. He runs His fingers through my hair, the same fingers that crocheted my soul together before I was born. The same hands that allow the pain I have felt for 7 years.

Schubert's *Ave Maria.* I discovered Barbara Bonney's version of it when I was only 10 or 11. I

54

didn't understand the German text, but I looked it up. The song was too beautiful to not understand what it meant. I remember having the flu around that age and listening to it for hours one day while napping and waiting for my dad to come pick up my brother and me. It helped me feel calm enough to sleep, even while miserable. It does the same for me now. I imagine the Blessed Mother was looking down at me from Heaven when I was little while I was napping in the same bedroom I still inhabit.

The dizziness. Everything spins. I feel like I'm on a ship, always rocking. Back and forth. Back and forth. Will the ship ever find its damn port? It'll find it once I die, I'll bet.

But that's okay. If God allows it, it means something. I know that very well. Sanctification is never easy, yet everyone must go through it. I can understand that this is how God wants me to draw closer to Him while also feeling every bit of pain from this illness and hating it. I hate it, but I didn't cause it, and there's no cure. The only way out is forward.

"Have thine own way, Lord!

Have thine own way!

Wounded and weary,

help me I pray!

Power, all power,

surely is thine!

Touch me and heal me,

Savior divine!"

Two Verses

Psalm 56:8 - "You keep track of all my sorrows. You have collected all my tears in your bottle. You have recorded each one in your book."

I first had a visual for this verse when I saw an item from my grandmother's bathroom sink moved to my mother's sink after she passed. It is a small bottle, perhaps only 4 inches tall and filled with water. It also has silver glitter floating in it so that when you tilt or shake it, the glitter floats, creating the idea that there are shining tears in it. On the front, there's a paper label with Psalm 56:8 in golden letters. Upon seeing it, it brought me back to the times when I was a teenager of about 16 or 17 and would talk to my grandmother, the only one I trusted in my family to really be able to speak to and not have to hold back certain details for fear of being told I was wrong or acting stupid. I remember telling her about my father, and how I would make myself sick from stress when I had to visit him on certain weekends. Walking on eggshells to appease him and acting in a specific way to make him look like the almighty figure he thinks he is would trigger debilitating migraines, which, of course, were then used as a weapon against me. "You're nauseous again? You know, you've just wasted all my money on this dinner. No, no, just take it home. It's fine. I'll give you some nausea medicine at home and then you can just go to bed if you want. I don't care," he'd say. Playing into his games was not an option. Apologizing only made it worse, because "You know what you're doing, it's always on purpose with you. You aren't stupid, I know that."

When my grandmother told me about that verse, I had been rambling to her about how that past weekend when I was at Dad's house, he took my brother and me to Animal Kingdom at Disney World. I have never liked Animal Kingdom, I don't know why. It was always very boring to me. My dad wanted to spoil and impress my soon-to-be stepmom, a woman he had known all their lives and had grown up with. If I enlightened you on how cold-hearted and malevolent (I do not use that word lightly when speaking about people!) she is, this would have to be published as a novel in multiple parts. I already had a migraine that day, and it was 95 degrees outside. This was during the years of wearing masks due to COVID concerns, and obviously, a black cloth mask trapped a lot of sweat. Then my stomach started hurting as well, and a vertigo spell started due to the heat. I had to put up with all of that for 8 hours. I tried my best to stay marginally polite, but my patience was wearing so thin. Once we got home, I wanted to go straight to bed. But my stepmom told me that Dad said a shower was necessary. That part I do understand, sweating for 8 hours does not impart pleasant smells. But after being in pain and ignored the whole day, I was irritated. I grumbled and got in the shower, and I hadn't been out for 10 minutes before my dad knocked and I let him in. He shut the door behind him with an amount of force that made me feel uneasy.

"What was your problem today?! You were acting so bitchy at the park. You totally humiliated me. Then we get home and when you're told to shower, you throw your phone (I tossed my phone onto the bed, and it landed by the wall and made a thudding sound. I did not throw it.) at the wall! That's the kind of behavior I'd expect from your brother, not you."

His face was red. His eyes were wide. I won't ever forget how his bluish-green eyes clashed with the anger of his skin. He looked like a monster, and I think in that moment, how he was inside was seeping out into his face. I still feel afraid and emotional writing this and having to remember what he said.

I cried. That's all I could do. Here I was, still in nothing but my bath towel, and he was screaming at me. He finished his insults and then pulled me in for a tight hug. He sniffled and seemed to cry, too, and he very well might have been. But I couldn't see his face to check if it was real. He said he'd give me 15 minutes and then would come back to talk. When he shut the door behind him, I clasped my hands to my mouth and tried to sob as quietly as I could. If I was heard crying, it would become a weapon. Nothing like how my Heavenly Father would treat me. If God could be so kind to me and not even be physically present, why couldn't my biological father do the same?

When Dad came back, he was calm again. I was still terribly upset and tearful. He sat next to me on the bed and now was being gentle and asking if anything was wrong earlier that day. Do take note of how he asked this after screaming abuse in my face while I was naked under a towel. I managed to choke and hiccup that I had been feeling sick all day and was already anxious because of a nightmare a few nights prior that I was having trouble forgetting. I don't remember what he said in reply, but he did say "You know, you're beautiful when you cry," as he wiped my tears so gently. That was the only time he'd ever comforted me like that, and it wasn't even genuine. He knew what he was doing; he knew if he wanted me to accept his apology, he had to act like he cared so deeply about me while I was still highly emotional.

Looking back with a clear head and freedom from him, I can almost feel my stomach twist thinking about how soft he was with me. You cannot tell me how beautiful I look when I cry while being the reason for my distress.

The next morning, I started to catch on that he did all that on purpose. By the time I got back to mom's house, and then my grandparent's house since they lived across the street, I was angry. I told my grandmother everything, much like I'm telling you now. And she listened to every detail in a manner I have yet to experience again from anyone else.

"The Bible says that God collects all our tears in a bottle and records them in His book," she said to me. I really can hear her voice telling me that again.

"Well, He's gonna have a lot of overfilled bottles for me, then," I'd dryly chuckle in response.

"I'm sure He has a lot of mine, too. But He collects them either way."

She didn't crack a usual joke in response, which meant that she wanted to make sure I was learning from what she was trying to say. And it took me this long to do so, but seeing that little plastic bottle of water and glitter along with knowing slightly better how suffering works in this world made that verse and her words finally click for me. I'm honored that God loves me enough to keep track of every tear I shed. Perhaps someday I can see how many bottles have my name on them.

Isaiah 43:2 - "When you pass through the waters, I will be with you; and when you pass through the rivers, they will not sweep over you. When you walk through the fire, you will not be burned; the flames will not set you ablaze."

It is human to forget, especially when one is in an altered mental state. I had been fighting with depression since I was 11 years old. I did not finally get treatment that worked until 19. I had forgotten the Psalm my grandmother showed me. I was so stuck in my darkness that any semblance of grace or love from God seemed totally impossible. I knew He loved me, but life was too hard. I just didn't care anymore. So I attempted suicide.

I didn't get very far before backing out and getting help at the hospital. I won't ever forget the help I was given there, and I especially will not forget the man who monitored me since I was a psychiatric patient. He was a very pleasant Haitian man named Lhomond. I remember him asking my name, and when I told him it was Faith, he said "Amen. That's a beautiful Godly name." That's when I knew God had put him there to meet me. I told him the story of how I got my name, how my mother had struggled to conceive and many doctors told her that she would never be able to have children. But she had a feeling that if she prayed, God would handle it in time. It took 6 years, but I was finally conceived. She said one day when she was in the shower, she heard a voice as clear as day tell her "Her name is Faith." She knew it wasn't my dad's voice. He wasn't even home. It sounded like

64

the voice came from inside the room, and she knew
the voice was God's. I just now asked my mother if
she knew my gender yet at that point, and her response
was "Yes, I knew. I'm a planner, I have to know." In
case anyone ever asks where I get my punctual quirks
from, the answer is right there.

My name is Faith because my mother had faith
that God would give her a child. I didn't say this out
loud to Lhomond, but I felt silly for letting myself
forget that whole story. I had forgotten that I am on
this earth because of the prayers of my mother and the
graces of God who knew me before I was born.

My grandmother had brought me my Bible
from home, and I was reading it in my hospital bed.
"If you don't mind, I'd like to ask you to turn to
chapter forty-three of Isaiah and read verses one
through five out loud," Lhomond requested. I started
to read; I didn't know what the chapter would say. But
as I went along reading, I was overcome with emotion
when I got to verse two. "When you pass through the
waters, I will be with you…" And I lost it. I broke

down crying, and he waited patiently by my bedside

for me to be able to continue, giving me as much time

as I needed. He understood as well as I did, if not more

than I did, that God was showing His love to me in

that verse, the love I was so desperate to feel but

somehow couldn't until right then. It was like the dam

had burst; His love was always there, building up, and

something broke. The water overflowed, and I was

soaked with every drop.

I wish I could remember how he explained one

of the following verses. He told me about God saying

"Because I love you," and explained how God's love

shows differently than our love between people does.

I'd like to add to his ability to turn four words into a

great lesson to be taught by bringing up Isaiah 43:2

once again. I re-read it yesterday, and I immediately

noticed how it says when you pass through the waters,

and through the rivers, and through the fire. Not when

God carries you over the pain and hurt. No, when *you*

pass through the hardships, He will be with you. He

knows that you are struggling, and He's always there,

but you have to be the one to get through the suffering. You have to take the steps.

See, God is not just keeping track of our suffering and then watching from a distance with His clipboard as we move through it. No, He is remembering our suffering and comforting us by doing so, and He is also right beside us as we walk. Much like a young child taking his first steps, God is our watchful Father who has His hands held out for us to grab if we stumble. He may only see it as a quick moment that our tiny hands grab for Him as we nearly fall over, but to us, having His hand to grab is everything. I'm alive and well today because His hand caught mine before I fell. All suffering has meaning, and God doesn't forget us, not even in our worst moments. As my friend Antoine told me recently when I really needed to hear it: "The path to Christ is suffering. It always has been suffering, and it's always hard to handle, but you've never escaped pain because you're made to endure pain. Whatever happens, remember what you're supposed to handle and why."

Face Forward

"You were an easy child. We never had to worry about you. Your brother, on the other hand.."

"All good children need to be spanked. You should be grateful we aren't bad parents; we don't hit you anywhere but the bottom."

"I only hit you because I love you. The Bible says 'Spare the rod, spoil the child.'"

These were all things I heard growing up. Sometimes I didn't understand why I was getting spanked. The spanking stopped for me at around 8 years old, but my brother got spanked until adolescence only because that's when he stopped crying while he got one. It got to a point where when we arrived back home at my grandparent's house after school, he'd get a spanking with the belt no matter how he acted that day. It was apparently because he was so poorly behaved all the time. My mother still tells the story of how she started spanking him when he was 4 months old—because he would kick her while getting his diaper changed. At his daycare, they saw bruises on his legs and bottom and called DCF. She still talks about how annoyed and angry she was that she had to take a day off work to let them in the house, not the fact that she hit my baby brother so hard over a reflex that he had multiple bruises.

Although I have very good memories of my grandmother and see her as my own mother in a way, I can't forget the memories of her spanking my brother after school. We'd get home and as soon as we put our backpacks down, she'd bring my brother into her room and spank him with that damn belt. I remember exactly how I'd run to the bathroom on the farthest end of the house and cover my ears as hard as I could to drown out his screaming. I'd try to cry as quietly as I could, not because she would get angry with me, but because she'd gently tell me it wasn't necessary for me to cry over my brother—"he deserved the spanking, after all." I'd whisper to myself, "it's okay, it's okay," over and over again. I'd count his spankings, which always were in the range of ten to twenty-three even if he was really good that day. She'd always tell him "I spank you because I love you" afterward, and I'd silently mouth "No you don't! If you loved him, you wouldn't make him cry like that!"

I remember thinking those words too when I would get spanked by my mother or father. I didn't dare say them out loud because that would earn me another spanking. I always preferred getting spanked by my mother—she used a wooden spoon, but was gentle enough to where it only stung badly. I dreaded being spanked by my father. He would make me pull my pants down and would spank me with such force I was nearly numb on my bottom. I never thought to check for bruises, so I don't know if I ever had any. I think I remember one of them saying that they spank me on the bottom because it's the only acceptable place to hit a child, and also because no one would ever see any marks if they were hidden by clothes.

Many people often say they got spanked and turned out fine. I can say with confidence that I did not. All it taught me was that my parents are not safe people and that I needed to be very careful around them.

Of course, once I turned 14, I became my mother's financial advisor and therapist. I was a child and then suddenly became an adult; there was no teenage experience for me. She would ask me if she should get a money order this week because we only had ten dollars for groceries, or if she should ask my grandparents if she could borrow money. I was acutely aware of how expensive her bills were and how awful my father was while they were married—they got divorced when I was seven, but long before that did our house feel empty. I noticed the emptiness back then, but as I think about it now, I also notice the sadness and fear that I thought was a normal part of life.

I grew to resent my father as a teenager, and looking back I wish I hadn't. She wasn't lying about what she said, but things are much worse now that my stepmother has established a codependent relationship with him and sees me, the daughter he had a part in making, as competition. I previously thought it wasn't possible for a narcissist to dominate another narcissist into putting a metaphorical leash on him, but she set the record for that.

My father didn't speak about my mother nicely either, but he would take jabs at her by talking down to me. When I would get irritated after he would provoke me by poking me, waving a hand in my face while I was sitting in the car's front passenger seat, or asking me a question and then making fun of me for my answer, he'd tell me "You're so grumpy, just like your mother." When he wasn't comparing me to someone he hated, he was using insults disguised as jokes toward my brother and I. One time, the three of us were at an ice cream shop we used to always go to. I don't remember what the topic of conversation was, but my father said "The only reason I feed you and give you a roof over your head every other weekend is because the law says I have to." My brother and I gave each other a look that said *"There's no way he really just said that."*

I learned then that being myself was not acceptable around my parents. My mother saw me as a convenient and free tool, and my father saw me as my mother. What if I just wanted to be myself and not get in trouble for it?

This dysfunctional family dynamic—what I've told you only scratches the surface—led me to a tricky relationship in my freshman year of high school. I was so in love with this boy who was a year older than me, but I'd never had any sort of steady love in my life; having undiagnosed autism added fuel to that fire as well. People decided they hated me before they knew anything about me past my name. I remember being on the playground in fourth grade, where a group of

my classmates were practicing a surprise birthday
song for our teacher that they would sing once we got
back to class. I wanted to be a part of it—I can hold a
tune very well and love to sing. When I approached
them and asked if I could be a part of the surprise, I
didn't even finish asking the question before they all
screamed at me to "go away, nobody wants you here."
Everything was conditional and transactional, so I
didn't notice that this boy in high school was only
flirting with me for fun and was also flirting with
multiple other girls. When we exchanged phone
numbers, he would text me when it was convenient for
him—which was usually once a month—and if I
didn't respond within the minute, he'd send me
multiple messages asking me if I was still there. By
the second semester of that year, he was asking me for
nude photos constantly, to the point of harassment.
He'd tell me what poses he wanted me to do in the
photos, and if I said no for any reason, he would say
"Oh, sorry.. I know I'm the worst person ever." My
naivety and kindness meshed together and I'd assure

him he wasn't what he said he was. Part of me back then wondered if I should just say that he was exactly what he said he was and block him—I should've listened to myself. It would've spared me an annoyance.

That was the year I got into witchcraft. I only did "healing magic" (as opposed to curses) and read tarot cards, but I also thought I could speak to deities directly and communicate with the dead. That was the time of my life where I held the utmost bitterness toward God. It greatly pains me to this day that I mocked Him and concluded that if He let me go through all of my trauma, then He clearly didn't care about me—and that Satan did. I am eternally grateful God led me out of that mess before there were any consequences.

I reverted back to Christianity at 16. Life was a little kinder to me at that time, and I'm grateful that I reverted back then before things got bad once more; I am confident that if I was not a Christian during the events that succeeded my high school graduation, I would have killed myself and wouldn't have tried to get help.

I disagree with the phrase "I'm not afraid of Hell; I've already experienced it on earth," not because I doubt people's experiences, but because anywhere on earth, God is with us. I absolutely agree however, with the rephrasing "I have experienced a portion of Hell on earth." In Hell, God is completely absent, which is a part of what makes it unbearable. On earth, evil reaches us little by little even if it hits us like a train. Hell has no buffer of good. We're blessed to get that buffer here.

If I believed the boldfaced lie that what we experienced or did in the past would follow us forever, I would now venture to say that I am a suicidal addict of self-harm and a secretively promiscuous Satanist witch. But none of those things are true; they ceased to be true when I reverted to Christianity and came back home to my Father's house to apologize. Now all I am known as is a daughter of the King of Kings. He blames me for nothing and wipes my tears when I cry to Him about all the things that have happened to me. He tells me "It's not your fault," and it's true. It's not my fault my parents didn't give me a safe place to be myself. It's not my fault I was taken advantage of and was asked for things I didn't want to do.

It's not your fault that you suffered abuse by the hands of people who were supposed to protect you and love you. Please do not beat yourself up over the actions of others toward you. You did *nothing* to deserve to be treated that way, and you are just as deserving of the love you may have never received. It will come to you in time, even if it simply comes from yourself. God's love is not reserved just for Christians. You are still a child of the Most High.

Where Is God When We Suffer?

"If God is real, why did bad things happen to me? Does God really love me if He could have stopped it?" This is a question that has been asked since the beginning of time precisely because it is so difficult to answer. Different people benefit from a different way of answering it. I will be attempting to take the empathetic and patient route from my own lived experience. Please note that I am not some great theologian with the perfect educated answer to everything; I hated school and was glad to graduate. Everything I say from this point on is said from life experience and from one healing heart to another.

I also won't be bothering with the "short answer" for this question, because there isn't one—not when one truly wants to answer it. To start, God is not just sitting above us, looking down from some cloud. He's everywhere, simultaneously sitting beside us and attending to all His children that are calling for Him.

That may make Him sound like a very busy God, but that's what omnipresence means. God being omnipresent means that He has not forgotten you when bad things happen to you.

Now, the matter of His omniscience would beg the question, "He knew that was going to happen to me and He just let it happen?" Yes, He knew that was going to happen to you, because He knows everything. That does not make Him indifferent. It's very easy for us to think that—and I often do—because we can't physically see Him. But He remembers the laws He made, and greatly disapproves when someone does something heinous towards another.

I also think there needs to be a change of perspective with how we tend to view God. All those beautiful old paintings show God the Father up in the clouds, looking down to us and us looking up to Him. But in some cases, that can lead to us thinking He is *only* in the clouds. That is where God's omnipresence comes in once again. He's not just up in the sky, He's everywhere. When we stroll through the park, He strolls with us to admire the birds—*His* birds—and enjoy the breeze. He watches over our shoulder as we write and He watches us paint to see all the colors take their place on the canvas. J.R.R. Tolkien spoke about "subcreation," where created beings like us create things themselves and actually take part in God's act of creation. But what about a sort of "supercreation," where subcreation becomes us imitating God in the same way a child likes to copy his father? His omnipresence would support that; we are everywhere in our created worlds, and He is everywhere in His.

As for His omnipotence in our suffering, that's part of why I mentioned that I don't like to imagine God just sitting on a cloud. I would be so angry to think that He sat in some cosmic armchair and looked down at me during my tempestuous childhood. I *was* angry to think that He was ignoring me, even after I reverted back to Christianity. It is perfectly okay for you to feel angry with God for what happened to you. He understands, truly, just like how a parent will let their teenager have time alone to calm down from anger after making a decision the teenager didn't like. It's just not good to be angry forever and reject Him for good. Part of healing is to let every emotion come. You've already dealt with shame that wasn't your fault, don't add to it by denying your whirlwind of emotions on the matter.

Besides, suffering is *necessary*. I wouldn't phrase it as a requirement, but it most certainly is inevitable. Suffering is holy—it is a strong tool of sanctification, even if we wish it wasn't. Sanctification is a lifelong journey where we are set apart and made holy, and if Christ suffered and died on the cross for us, then that is a part of holiness. That doesn't make it easy. I don't want this to sound like I'm telling you to toughen up or just pray more—I will do no such thing. There's no point in making the suffering more unbearable through a lack of empathy.

And don't let anyone brush off your pain by implying you're doubting God. Suffering *is* a part of His plan, because it has a purpose. It's not mindless lollygagging. But God isn't laughing at our tears, and although our rejoicing in the face of suffering pleases Him greatly, He knows how hard that is to do when you feel like you can't go on. When we sit in our chairs and sob uncontrollably, He kneels beside us and puts a hand on our shoulder. He does not let go until He is sure we feel at least a little better.

God is not watching the opera of our lives from private box seats. He produced the show and is directing it. Every stage entrance and exit, every intermission, every emotional aria, it is all His work. He rejoices when we rejoice and He weeps alongside us when we weep. And we should live to see His standing ovation, even if we don't agree with every staging arrangement.

And often, we must be content with not having answers to everything. In God's eyes, we are infants even if we live past one hundred. If He told us every secret of the universe and every reason for His choices, we'd die—we wouldn't be able to handle that knowledge. So leave it up to the one who *can* handle it.

As I close out this essay collection, I have included Job 38 and Job 40:2 below as well as a personal prayer I wrote because I feel they prove the point of the previous paragraph. Job wanted answers about his suffering, and he got none—he was instead challenged on his knowledge of the world versus God's. It's almost as if God was saying, "Listen to all of the knowledge I have of the earth and the universe I created. Do you not think that if I know all of these things, I should know the meaning of why you suffer?"

Job 38 and 40:2 - "Then the LORD spoke to Job out of the storm. He said:

'Who is this that obscures my plans
with words without knowledge?
Brace yourself like a man;
I will question you,
and you shall answer me.

*Where were you when I laid the earth's
foundation?
Tell me, if you understand.
Who marked off its dimensions? Surely you
know!
Who stretched a measuring line across it?
On what were its footings set,
or who laid its cornerstone—
while the morning stars sang together
and all the angels shouted for joy?
Who shut up the sea behind doors
when it burst forth from the womb,
when I made the clouds its garment
and wrapped it in thick darkness,
when I fixed limits for it
and set its doors and bars in place,
when I said, 'This far you may come and no
farther;
here is where your proud waves halt'?
Have you ever given orders to the morning,
or shown the dawn its place,*

that it might take the earth by the edges
and shake the wicked out of it?

The earth takes shape like clay under a seal;
its features stand out like those of a garment.

The wicked are denied their light,
and their upraised arm is broken.

"Have you journeyed to the springs of the sea
or walked in the recesses of the deep?

Have the gates of death been shown to you?
Have you seen the gates of the deepest darkness?

Have you comprehended the vast expanses of
the earth?
Tell me, if you know all this.

What is the way to the abode of light?
And where does darkness reside?

Can you take them to their places?
Do you know the paths to their dwellings?

Surely you know, for you were already born!
You have lived so many years!

Have you entered the storehouses of the snow
or seen the storehouses of the hail,

which I reserve for times of trouble,
for days of war and battle?
    What is the way to the place where the
lightning is dispersed,
    or the place where the east winds are scattered over
the earth?
    Who cuts a channel for the torrents of rain,
and a path for the thunderstorm,
    to water a land where no one lives,
an uninhabited desert,
    to satisfy a desolate wasteland
and make it sprout with grass?
    Does the rain have a father?
Who fathers the drops of dew?
    From whose womb comes the ice?
Who gives birth to the frost from the heavens
    when the waters become hard as stone,
when the surface of the deep is frozen?
    Can you bind the chains of the Pleiades?
Can you loosen Orion's belt?

*Can you bring forth the constellations in their
seasons*
   or lead out the Bear with its cubs?
   Do you know the laws of the heavens?
Can you set up God's dominion over the earth?
   Can you raise your voice to the clouds
and cover yourself with a flood of water?
   Do you send the lightning bolts on their way?
Do they report to you, 'Here we are'?
   Who gives the ibis wisdom
or gives the rooster understanding?
   Who has the wisdom to count the clouds?
Who can tip over the water jars of the heavens
   when the dust becomes hard
and the clods of earth stick together?
   Do you hunt the prey for the lioness
and satisfy the hunger of the lions
   when they crouch in their dens
or lie in wait in a thicket?

Who provides food for the raven

when its young cry out to God

and wander about for lack of food?

Will the one who contends with the Almighty
correct Him?

Let him who accuses God answer Him!"

Closing Prayer

Thank you, God, for allowing me to feel pain. Through this pain, be it physical, spiritual, or emotional, I am granted just a mere glimpse into what Christ bore so that I might live. This pain might often be much too overwhelming, and it may feel like too much for me to handle, but it's never more than You can handle. When I am in pain and need to rest, it gives me time to reflect on Christ's sacrifice for me. I am being cared for by the Great Physician, and I am not afraid.

www.ingramcontent.com/pod-product-compliance
Lightning Source LLC
Chambersburg PA
CBHW021333160726
47994CB00007B/2674